WHAT OTHERS ARE SAYING

"This book is one of the most well written books by a Viet-nam veteran I have ever read. It is well documented with excellent photographs and concise language. The harsh realities of one soldier's journey is well written, straightforward and emotionally moving. This is a 'tell it like it was' book by a true American hero. The personal documentation by the author of his time 'in country' is absolutely the most realistic, authentic tale ever written about that time in our American history. As I read this book it brought back with extreme clarity memories of my own official mission in that time and region.

A highly recommended read.

-- *Dennis Lacey,*
U. S. Navy veteran, U. S. Secret Service (Ret.)

"George Graves served honorably and heroically during the Vietnam War and has written a compelling first person account of daily life and combat action during that conflict. *A Soldier's Journey* brings to life the sights, sounds, and emotions of a controversial war."

-- *Larkin Spivey*
Lt. Col. U. S. Marine Corps (Ret.)

See more recommendations on Page 116.

*Writing this journey
was not for the telling,
but for the hearing.*

A Soldier's Journey

A Story of Vietnam

by

George Graves

Pp
Prose Press

A Soldier's Journey: A Story of Vietnam

Second edition 2015
photos added, 2021

Comments: Contact George Graves,
asoldiersjourney@hotmail.com

If you would like to add to this book,
see page 116 for more information.

ISBN: 978-0-9886194-8-7

Cover/Interior Design: OBD
proseNcons@live.com

Published by Prose Press
Pawleys Island,
South Carolina 29585

proseNcons@live.com

DEDICATION

My dad was in the Philippines during World War II, in the army. All of them were heroes in those days in all branches of the service; all were heroes who fought valiantly in that war for the freedom we have today. He only talked about it to me on a few rare occasions, before my return from Vietnam. Once I had asked him what had happened to the first joint knuckles on his right hand; they were scarred as if they had been skinned off long ago. He said the slide and bolt of his weapon (.30 caliber M-1 carbine) blew out while he was firing it on a patrol and part of it or part of the wooden stock took the skin off his knuckles. He was in a cavalry unit, the "acting" supply sergeant when he wasn't on guard duty or patrol. His actual rank was corporal. After I got home from VN he was more open about his WWII experiences but I think it was just for my benefit. He passed away in 1999 and I wished we had talked more about his experiences.

So to my dad and for all the "brothers," thanks. All gave some, some gave all.

I'm also writing this journey not for the telling, but for the hearing, by any of my family who might wish they had heard more about my experiences, like I wish I had from my dad.

ACKNOWLEDGEMENTS

All the events in this journal are described to the best of my memory after almost 45 years; I am now 70. If you were there and were part of these events and have anything to add or change, please let me hear from you. All the pictures except for some of the ones I'm in were taken by me, and some of these were taken with a shutter delay with the camera sitting on something. All the pictures were sent home undeveloped and I didn't take a good look at them for about five years. About four years ago, in 2008, my brother-in-law, Lee Lacey, put the pictures on a CD ROM and a DVD. My son Chris's girlfriend at the time (now wife), Dani, showed me how to use a program to restore these pictures. I restored more than 230 slides, plus many more stills obtained from five rolls of super 8 mm film, this past December (2011). Every picture told a story or part of one; without these I probably would not have remembered half of the entries.

Thanks also to Bob Swieder for help making the stills from the movies.

The format of Larkin Spivey's "Stories of Faith and Courage from World War II / Battlefields & Blessings," and looking at my pictures while I was restoring them helped prompt me to write this journey.

Also, some prodding since returning from VN, and more lately, by William "Burke" Hicks, (the first friend I made in the eighth grade when my family moved to Hickory, also now a poet and short story writer), helped me make the decision to do this.

A special thanks to Landis Bargatze and Gary Anthony and for the pertinent information they provided.

Thanks to Joe Ruisi for insight after reading the first draft. Most importantly, to my wife Lacey whose help in using a computer to write with, starting at the beginning with how to turn it on, I couldn't have done without.

I started the first draft on Jan. 1, 2012, and finished it, with most pictures selected, by the first week in April, after many more weeks of struggling with presentation and other things. Thanks for the support from many others not mentioned, by Aug. 20, 2012. The following is the result.

Dad 1944

CONTENTS

1
INTRODUCTION

"Walk worthy of the calling with which you were called."
— Eph. 4:1

The journey starts with my draft notice, then a little about basic training followed by AIT (advanced infantry training), departure to VN, "in country" experiences, and ends with departure from Cam Ranh, VN. (AIT was in Tiger-land; most, if not all, of the GIs who went through AIT at Tiger-land were assigned to a line company or some other unit in VN that exposed them to a combat environment during most, if not all, of their entire tour of duty in VN.) My journey was a little different, but not much.

1

2
INDUCTION

"In his heart a man plans his course, but the Lord determines his steps."
—Pro. 16:9

Early in 1966, a notice arrived from my favorite uncle. "…you have been … please report … the induction center at … in Charlotte, N.C. ... for your physical exam…" Memory fails me on the exact wording, but you get the message – I got the message. Having just celebrated a 24th birthday, married for a short period (no children and none on the way), and about three years into my career, drafted.

I sincerely believe everyone should spend at least two years in some military branch of service, I just wasn't expecting it this "late" in life. My induction was delayed six weeks for some medical reason I'm not remembering, while the rest of the guys who also went down there went on to basic training. Gary Anthony, who is mentioned later in one of the episodes, was one of these. Six weeks later I returned; this time my youngest brother Lee Graves came with me because he had by then heard from his favorite uncle, too. However, he was held up for six weeks for medical reasons, as I had been, while I got to go to Fort Bragg for basic training. Lee came back six weeks later and was inducted then.

Walter Graves, the "middle" brother, had tried to join the Navy many years earlier after high school but had been turned down and reclassified as 4F. The only excitement during induction came when a Marine recruiter sergeant came through the line, picking every fifth man for the Marines. "…I thought they came out of the Navy…" Anyway, being fourth in line, I didn't get picked; however, this was my first exposure to volunteering.

Local InductioCenter ?

3
BASIC WAS BASIC

Get up early, early-early, into fatigues, run to the mess hall for breakfast to practice more standing in line, eat, then more physical exercises of all types, run 'til you throw up, then go eat lunch, and start all over again.

Some days we got acquainted with different weapons, taking them apart, putting them back together, sometimes in the dark. We had to learn the rules and regulations that make the Army what it is. We learned to work as a team; this started with marching while carrying a telephone pole, remember. This worked; by the time we finished we actually started looking good at marching. Looking good while carrying a telephone pole was even more amazing. To tell you the truth, I liked it. If I'd been 18 when I was drafted and didn't have a job waiting, and lived through Vietnam, I could have made a career of it.

Now I don't remember what you had to make to pass the final PT (physical training) test at basic, but 500 was the max. A very few did max it. I made 475, losing 25 points on the last test trying to run a mile in six minutes in combat boots. My time was six minutes and 25 seconds. However, we all passed and got our orders for our next duty station; for me, Tiger-land, Fort Polk, La.

4
ARRIVAL/TIGER-LAND/AIT
(Jan. 3 – March 8, 1967)

"…but there is a friend who sticks closer than a brother."
—*Pro. 18:24*

Tiger-land was part of Fort Polk, La. AIT is advanced infantry training. Tiger-land meant you were going to Vietnam. Sorry, no cooks, clerks, mechanics, medics, etc., were invited to Tiger-land. Some of us at basic must have been special because not everyone at basic got to go there. We were there for "jungle warfare" training.

There were ninety-three of us in my unit (A Company, 3rd Battalion, 3rd Brigade); five of us were 24 or 25, the rest were teenagers. By the time we left, everyone, including some of the instructors who were younger than us, was calling the five of us "the old guys." Funny how circumstances change the meaning of things, isn't it?

I think it was around midnight when I got checked in and pointed toward my barracks. There was a one bulb, shaded light outside over the door that didn't let much light into the building. When you went in you couldn't see much of anything past the first bunk beds on each side except that the first bunks on each side looked empty. There was snoring coming from the back. I set my duffle bag down and climbed into the top bunk on the right as quickly and quietly as possible and was almost asleep with my back to the door when I heard someone coming through the door. As I turned over, I noticed this someone was coming through the door taking off a pair of sunglasses and sporting two black eyes with stitches under one of them.

"Sunglasses," I said.

"Don't say anything more or you'll need them tomorrow," he said.

I laughed, then he laughed, then someone said "shut up." I pointed to the bunk below and whispered "tomorrow." He said his name was (Landis) Bargatze and he would see me in the morning. The next morning, however, before "revelry" (reveille) someone woke me up and took me down to the motor pool to get a driver's license. Landis told me later that day that going to get my license saved my life. We both laughed again and this was the start of becoming good friends. He was one of the old guys, too. Another one of the old guys we met the next day was Jimmy Pruitt. All three of us became the best of friends by the end of AIT. These were the only two from our AIT unit who I ran into in VN before I got to Cam Ranh on the way home.

Weekend pass

5
TIGER-LAND

We were issued M-14s in Tiger-land but were told the weapon we most likely would be issued "in country" was the M-16. We became familiar with an assortment of other weapons: shoulder-fired grenade and rocket launchers; machine guns; claymore mines; and mortars, to mention most of them. Most important, to me, were the field exercises where we were given a compass and turned loose into the woods to find our way somewhere and then find our way back.

The company was always marched to the exercises, where we were sometimes divided into smaller groups. I got to ride behind, following the company, driving a jeep ambulance,

Standing: St. Onge, Parker, Austine, Bargatze and Graves; sitting: Pichardo.

7

which led to me catching a lot of "flak," as you can imagine.

On one exercise, we were divided into small groups, eight if my memory is right, and were sent out to locate an enemy village and to look for a tunnel that led to it. After we found the village, we circled around it until we found an entrance to an underground tunnel. It turned out to be about the size of a manhole cover and was well camouflaged.

We then looked to see where a tunnel might come up in the village, like a well, which it did. Next we had to try and calculate the distance to the middle of the village because we were going to have to go down in the tunnel
– I think it was about six feet underground – and try and come up in the village. It looked like it was about fifty to sixty yards to the middle of the village. We were told that in Vietnam the tunnels could split and not all exits would come up in a village and some of the tunnels were big enough to sit up in and sometimes stand up in. Also, he said in VN this job was done by volunteers called "tunnel rats." Before we went down we had to decide who was going first. I'm claus-trophobic so I asked the instructor if I could go first or last – I didn't want to be in the middle. I caught hell for just opening my mouth. He also didn't hesitate to tell me that I would go first, my second experience with volunteering.

After we entered the tunnel, we went through as quickly as possible. We passed at least two of what we thought could be exit holes before we decided we had come far enough to go up. I was glad all these decisions were team decisions. Sadly, we found we had crawled all the way to the other side of the village. We had to go back down and try again but before we did we took another look at the distance and this time, taking it a little slower, we came up where we were supposed to, in the well.

There were times when things didn't turn out exactlyr-ight for jungle training. We were on a night-time exercise simulating holding a hill-top position. It was late January or early February and we were wearing what should have been sufficient clothing for Fort Polk, La.; however, what felt like a record cold snap came in that night. The water in the cap of our canteens froze and we were literally "shaking in our boots."

On the last training day at Tiger-land, all the units "graduating" met in a large auditorium for a "farewell" address. The part that stuck in my mind the most was at the end when we were asked to look at whoever was sitting beside us because if they could get us back here in one year the person on each side of us would be missing. I was sitting between Jimmy and Landis.

Front - Ed Chrolot, Thomas Goff, George Graves, Ira Rice, Landis,Bargatze, and Bill Austine, Dwight Fox
2nd row – Jimmy Pruitt and Albert Parker.

6
FORT DIX, NJ, TO VIETNAM
(March 31, 1967)

On March 31, 1967, ninety-one of the ninety-three Tiger-land grads had orders to leave from Fort Dix for Vietnam. One was going to OCS (Officer Candidate School) and would come over later, the other was going to Germany with a deferment because of a family member who was already in VN. (My brother Lee was given a deferment, because I was on my way to VN when he finished his basic training.)

The plane looked like it was big enough to carry ninety people; however, I don't think all of the guys on the plane were from our AIT unit. There were only seven windows in the passenger section and the three of us were seated in the middle of the plane so we didn't get to see any of the scenery. I was sitting in the middle again between Jimmy and Landis. To pass the time, we played poker when we got tired of listening to music through our earphones. The music consisted of about twelve songs continually repeating. We must have heard "I Heard it through the Grapevine" by Gladis Knight and the Pips a couple of hundred times before we reached VN. We played more than 300 hands of poker – no betting, just keeping track of who won each hand. I don't remember who won but I think it ended up with one hand difference between the three of us.

We made a few stops on the way: California, Honolulu,and Okinawa. They let us off the plane in Honolulu but confined us to an area in a lounge. The first time we ordered a pitcher of beer we realized there were only a few of us old enough to buy beer. Several of us got away with buying about eight more pitchers before someone caught on and cut us off.

When we got to Okinawa we picked up a fighter escort the rest of the way to Vietnam. Needing an escort and no way to see out if something happened gave me my first little case of the "willies" as I thought about it, kind of like when the hair stands up on your neck for a couple of seconds, or how a long-tailed cat feels when he first enters in a room full of rocking chairs.

Base Camp

Dragon Mountian

7
90TH REPLACEMENT, BIEN HOA , VN
(April 2-26, 1967)

We were marched from the plane to a bus and from the bus to check in at the "90th Repel-Depel." The next morning after breakfast, we fell out into an assembly area where all new personnel would receive their next duty station assignment. We were told we could be here for about ten to fourteen days before receiving our duty orders; my duty station orders didn't come early. After this roll call we were told to stay in the area for work detail placement. Once you were placed on a work detail you would stay on the same detail until you got your duty station orders.

Jimmy and Landis got picked for details right away, after this I only saw them at night and they both got their next duty station call in about ten days. I only saw each one once again, separately, before Cam Rhan. A fellow standing beside me, after Jimmy and Landis got picked for a detail, told me to follow him over to where he was to be picked up for his detail. If someone got their duty orders they would need replacements on the detail and this was the easiest detail here, he said. You sweep out officers' "hooches," then keep out of sight until supper time. I decided to take a chance because you were going to get picked for something, this was not really volunteering.

"Sure 'nuff," an officer came to get him and some others and needed a few more and picked me as one. He was right; the officers were gone all day and all we did was sweep and "hang low" until time to eat, lunch and then supper. I did not see anyone I came over with after about ten days. Unbelievably, my duty station orders didn't come for about 24 days.

The only excitement came was while I was eating lunch in the mess hall one day. I was trying to get a soy sauce bottle open and tapped the cap a few times on the edge of the table trying to loosen it up. Then, giving it a good twist – it looked like a little Listerine bottle – the top broke off, just below the cap, probably from tapping it. I threw it in the trash and went on eating.

Very shortly after, I noticed a drop of blood on the side of my tray. I held my hands up, palms away, but didn't see anything, palms facing, still nothing. I took another bite then noticed another drop. Again, same procedure, palms out then palms in, seeing nothing until my palms were facing me and I folded my fingers down and then facing me, third finger, first joint, right hand, was a knuckle bared to the bone. I was now beginning to feel a little sting. I straightened my finger out quickly and left the mess hall for the aid station.

There was a "spec four" on duty so I showed him my finger and explained what happened. He told me all the doctors were out to lunch and asked would I mind if he sewed it up. I said sure, but I felt like I was volunteering again, especially when he gave me six shots of Novocain, three on each side of the knuckle. My worst wasp sting didn't hurt as much as each one of these shots. I was lying on my back, my hand across my chest on top of a towel, another towel over my arm with a hole in it exposing my hand, so I just closed my eyes waiting for my finger to get numb.

"Yeow, what are you doing?" I yelled.

"I'm sewing it up," the aide replied.

"Well, it ain't numb yet," I retorted. I laid my head back down waiting for him to put the splint on, which he said would keep me from bending it.

"Yeow, what are you doing now?" I yelled again.

"It needed two stitches," he said.

No, you don't get a purple heart for that, but he came close.

The day finally came when I got my duty station orders to 1st Battalion, 22nd Infantry of the 4th Infantry Division.

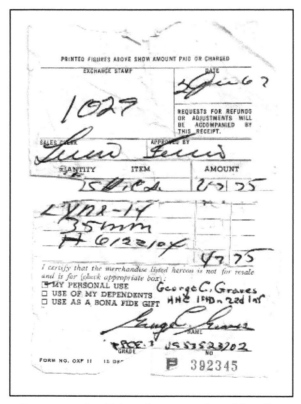

Camera receipt. This is the camera I used for all the pictures in this book.

8
BASE CAMP

The 4th Division Base Camp, located in Pleiku Province, in the central highlands, was the largest Army base camp in VN. It was approximately one square mile. The 1/22nd was located on the east perimeter in about the middle of the base with no one between it and the base camp perimeter bunkers and the perimeter wire. One plane ride and one truck ride deposited six of us in front of the S-1 of the 1/22nd.

The S-1 was the office of the battalion officers and all the company clerks. It sat on the northwest corner of our area, at an intersection, with a sandbagged bunker, the supply room, aid station, two latrines, billets for A, B, C, and D company, the recon platoon base camp personnel,

Looking east from behind S-1.

15

Looking east from behind the mess hall.

and the shower, stretching east down the street toward the perimeter. South of the S-1 was the mess hall, then stretching east of the mess hall, toward the perimeter, were the commissioned and upper non-commissioned officers' quarters, another sandbagged bunker, and the S-5 and the S-4 tents. I don't remember exactly where the communication shop and the motor pool were located. The S-1 and mess hall were all wooden buildings, the rest were either tents or tents with wooden frames to be converted to all wooden buildings as soon as possible.

However, as soon as we "de-trucked" we were told to drop our bags and fall in. Someone asked if anyone could type, no one raised their hand so guess what, yep, I "volunteered" again. After a quick test, to see if I really could type, I was told to type in the information requested on a card given to each of us. We were then sent to check out a weapon and return immediately.

Then we were told we were going on a five- to seven-day patrol in a relatively safe area to get familiar with the

16

environment. This is when I learned I was allergic to government-issued insect repellant. I broke out in hives, some bigger than a quarter, and spent sleeping time for the rest of my tour under a poncho liner to keep from getting eaten alive. When we returned from this patrol we could expect to be assigned to a line company and given an orientation on what was going on with each company. Each line company contained about 120 men in the field, the recon patrol about ninety. However, we were returned to our company area from this patrol after four days.

When we got off the truck in front of the S-1 we were told we had been called in early because C Company had been in a fire fight, somewhere near the 3 Tango fire base, and needed a lot of replacements. We were to wait here for another truck to take us to a chopper pad. All available personnel from base camp and from the Oasis, a resupply camp, would be sent out to the fire base at 3 Tango, which had been depleted sending help out to C Company. At 3 Tango, C Company was described as being "non-combatant," as a company, because of the number of casualties.

Back of S-1

9
3 TANGO

"Precious in the sight of the Lord is the death of
His godly ones."
—Psalms 116:15

This fire base, called 3 Tango, was located just barely in
VN at the border between Cambodia and Laos. It was a little
bigger than two football fields. It contained an operations
center, artillery pieces (usually 105 "howitzers"), one or
more mortar batteries, support vehicles (tanks), and troops.
We arrived in a CH 47

Taken from a Huey helicopter.

Chinook helicopter, a supplies and troop carrier, into a potentially "hot LZ," (a landing zone possibly under fire). We would not be landing but would "deplane" by jumping off the ramp at the back end of the Chinook as it hovered moving slightly forward. Fortunately, there wasn't any ground fire while we "deplaned" and ran for cover. However, a few nights later we received our "baptism of fire." As soon as we all were inside the perimeter we were checked in and then assigned a bunker to man. At first we – a fellow who went by Tiny and a Cajun named Eddie and myself – were brought to a bunker that was full of ammo, without a roof on it. Fortunately, the S-4 officer, Capt. Ashe, was standing there and said it was being rebuilt and no personnel would be staying in it anyway. Tiny and I were moved to another bunker. Eddie joined us each night as we rotated on guard duty at the bunker. We set up our claymores on our perimeter and hooked them up to the hand generators inside the bunker. However, we had to pull guard duty outside the bunker to be able to see all the area in front of the bunker. This was fine by me; in fact, I spent most of my time outside that bunker

Taken from a Huey helicopter.

because it was just too small. (I soon got over that small bunker phobia.)

It was a few days later, at the end of my watch, about 2 a.m., when the attack started. Tiny was crawling out through the hole in the side of our bunker to relieve me when we both heard the click-click of outgoing mortar fire and it wasn't coming from behind us. He quickly backed up and I came in right behind him just as the first air burst went off. The fight went on for a while but no one got past the perimeter and the only man we lost was on LP (listening post). Often at night men are sent out beyond the perimeter into different areas as LPs to radio any enemy movement in their area. This night one was killed by our own fire while he was trying to slip back through the perimeter. The only information we heard was that he knew his orders to go home were in. I can't imagine that he didn't radio he was coming in; possibly not everyone got the message. You weren't supposed to come in until you were given an "all's clear" after the perimeter was notified to watch for you.

10
ROLLING THUNDER

Several times while at 3 Tango we had to vacate our bunkers because B-52s were going to be carpet bombing close enough to shake down a bunker. Even when you couldn't see the planes, you could see the smoke, feel the ground shake, hear, and sometimes see the explosions. This was the first time I realized the enemy didn't always have the home-field advantage.

11
NOW HEAR THIS

Often, daily and nightly, the artillery battery at 3 Tango would engage in a little harassing and interdicting fire, called H & I, firing rounds into areas where enemy movement was known to persist. Our 105s were located close to the middle of the fire base.

One night after coming off my turn on watch at the bunker, I walked back toward the middle of the fire base to where one of the "relief" canisters was placed in the ground, right in front of one of the 105s. I always thought that this was a lot safer than whizzing on the perimeter at night. I was standing with my back to the 105 battery when one of the

105 Battery

guys said they were getting ready to fire some H & I. I turned my head to the right and told them I was hurrying; however, before I could turn back they fired a round over my head. I didn't remember much until the next morning and all I could hear was a train going through my head.

I was sent back to base camp to the aid station at 1/22nd where I was told my right ear drum was ruptured and I might have a concussion. From here I was to go to the 6th Field Hospital at Qui Nhon.

12
A STOP ALONG THE WAY

"Heal me, O Lord, and I shall be healed; Save me, and I shall be saved."
—Jer. 17:14

On the way to Qui Nhon, I had to go through what seemed to be an "emergency" hospital at the air base at Pleiku. The waiting room must have been the same for both because while waiting for my flight, someone, a doctor or aide, came in from the adjoining emergency room looking for help. I had seen an ambulance and another truck pull in. He asked me and another GI to go with this other person who was with him (both of them were wearing white uniforms) and bring back anything he handed us.

The other guy told us a Lambretta, a three-wheeled mo-
torcycle with a passenger "cage," full of Vietnamese had run
over a mine. A building outside the emergency room was
their blood bank: It looked like a restaurant's refrigerated
food locker, a metal building about 20 feet by 20 feet. Whatever he handed us we ran back with.

When we got there, another ambulance had arrived with
GIs from a "deuce-and-a-half" that had also run over a mine.
Before we left to make another run; we were told to bring
whatever we could into the next room beside the emergency
room because they had just received a "medevac" call that a
chopper was coming in now with a GI who had a "sucking"
chest wound and everyone in the emergency room was being
moved.

We got back just as the GI was being brought in on a
stretcher. Most of his shirt had been cut off and a medic was
holding a piece of plastic over a bullet wound in his chest.
One more trip to the blood bank then the doctor sent us back
out to the waiting room. Shortly my ride was available but
I couldn't get out of my mind how focused those medical
people were in the midst of multiple emergencies.

13
GOING BACK HOME

"Great are Your tender mercies, O Lord..."
—Psalms 119:156a

At the 6th Field Hospital in Qui Nhon, they checked out my ears and said they couldn't find any serious problems. I would probably suffer from tinnitus, ringing in the ear, but my hearing would come back close to normal soon. Feeling I had been flown around needlessly, considering how minor my condition now seemed to be, it made me think that every GI must get the best attention available, especially after seeing what was done for those GIs in Pleiku.

The ride back to 1/22nd was in a C-130, a four- motor plane used to carry vehicles and supplies. While approaching An Khe, an engine was shot out by ground fire. The plane couldn't land there or anywhere else in this area because the runways were too short to land without being able to reverse the pitch of the props on all four engines (to help slow down). We had to go down to Cam Rhan. I was stuck there sleeping on a bench in the waiting room for two days and couldn't leave the air base because I didn't have a travel or leave order to be there or to go anywhere else. Fortunately, someone at 1/22nd caught up with me and got me a ride back "home."

14
OASIS

On returning to base camp, orders were cut making me a mail clerk and sending me to the Oasis as a forward clerk until a replacement came in with that MOS (military occupation). This lasted from six to eight weeks, I don't remember exactly.

The Oasis was a resupply camp for a large number of 4th Division and other units. I don't know how many other units were out there but I could see more than 100 people being there. Our area, 1/22nd, consisted of tents for the CO (commanding officer), XO (executive officer), COMMO shop, motor pool, and at least two other tents that were not occupied during my time there. Most of the time there were only six to eight other people from 1/22nd out there, mostly motor

Company area oasis

pool and communications personnel, and neither the CO nor the XO came out during this time, either. I don't remember whose mess hall we ate in.

I stayed in the XO's tent while there because it was also the mail room. Regular duties included typing a daily morning report, mail call, night-time guard duty, typing requests from people here or sent in from people out with the line companies and the recon platoon, and rarely a one-day only (out and back) flight to a line company or the recon platoon. Irregular duties were pulling guard duty in the day time and going to see the doughnut dollies when they came around to play games and serve coffee and doughnuts, a nice change in the scenery.

An aerial view of the company area.

The XO's tent.

15
NO MAIL

On one occasion, at the Oasis, I had to pull guard duty during the day, night time was pretty regular but this was a first for the day time. The mail didn't get posted or delivered that day; the result was no happy campers. I thought I'd never hear the end of it – getting shot sounded like relief. I never even caught this much flak when I was driving the ambulance at AIT. All was forgiven when someone confirmed I was really on guard duty and not at the doughnut dolly's tent all day. Neither rain nor snow nor guard duty during the day stopped the mail from getting delivered after that, due to a note from my XO to the local warden, or whoever was in charge of day-time guard duty.

The doughnut dolly tent.

16
MOTOR POOL RATS

*"The quiet words of the wise are more to be heeded than
the shouts of a ruler of fools."*
—Ecc. 9:17

The motor pool tent, "dispatcher," at the Oasis, was located beside the XO tent. It was manned and lived in by the motor pool sergeant and two mechanics/ drivers and was the closest occupied tent to mine. Therefore, I spent a lot of the time there at night, when I wasn't on guard duty, until hitting the sack. On most occasions we'd play cards but also a lot of the time would be spent reading mail, the Stars & Stripes, talking about home, or just "shooting the breeze."

The motor pool sergeant.

Sometimes we worked on the rat population. The Oasis was one of the oldest of resupply camps around. Resupply camps usually have to move for sanitary reasons more than anything else, but the Oasis had been there a long time and was still there when I left. The floor in the motor pool tent was made from wooden shell boxes turned upside down. Walking on them

had popped out some knot holes and occasionally a rat would come up through them. They could get in plenty of other ways and usually confined their traffic to the top of the sand bags that were about three feet high and went around the inside wall of their tent.

When they came up through the floor it sometimes became a challenge as to who had the right-of-way. They had a small dog also but it was smaller than the rats. They even took turns sleeping with the dog to keep it off the floor. One way they tried to get rid of the rats was with cheese, blasting caps, and a hand generator (from their claymores) but some officer got wind of this and frowned on that procedure.

17
HO CHI MINH'S REVENGE

*"Be kindly affectionate to one another with brotherly love,
in honor giving preference to one another; not lagging
in diligence, fervent in spirit, serving the Lord; rejoicing
in hope, patient in tribulation, continuing steadfastly in
prayer; distributing to the needs of the saints, given to
hospitality."*
—Rom. 12:10-13

Also referred to as the "green apple quick step," you knew when it hit the Oasis because there would be a lot of extra, fast-moving traffic to the latrines. Most latrines were called "three-holers" (having three places to sit), "out houses," or "johns."

While I was in flight to the "john" one day I heard someone else running, coming up fast behind me. When I went through the door I grabbed the door frame on the right side and swung out of the way. "Big Swede" came through the door turning backwards and sat down on the hole in the middle of the bench with his pants between his knees and his hips. He said he didn't make it so I handed him my knife. He cut his pants off and stuffed them down in the can. It's hard to keep your cheeks pinched together while running fast.

P.S.: The knife had belonged to one of my wife's uncles, Bill Jones, a retired W-4, (Chief Warrant Officer), in the Secret Service during World War II and Korea. He offered it to me just before I left for VN and said he hoped I might find a good use for it.

18
A CHANCE MEETING

One morning while walking toward the PX at the Oasis, I noticed a GI coming toward me carrying cases of beer stacked so high he couldn't see where he was going. I asked if I could help him, he said sure so I grabbed the top two cases. That's when I recognized him. It was Jimmy Pruitt, one of the "old guys" from Tiger-land. He said his PC (personal carrier) was about 50 yards down the road. The rest of his crew was there.

When we got there, we sat down for a couple of hours

A personal carrier

and had a reunion over a case of beer. One topic was who we had seen. He said he hadn't seen Landis but had seen a few others from AIT. Another topic of "lesser" importance but still noteworthy was the quality of beer here. We both noted that canned beer was much better, but leave the bottled beer alone. I remarked that on one occasion, off base, I had noticed while the bottled beers' labels were the same, the caps were of different colors. Never drink bottled beer in VN. It was the worst tasting "beer" I ever tried; I hope it wasn't recycled. I couldn't finish it. You can recap a bottle but you can't reseal a can.

19
OASIS TO BASE CAMP
"Give careful thought to your ways."
—Hag. 1:5

The COMMO shop sent word that base camp had called ordering me to catch a ride on a convoy going to base camp. I was to catch a ride in a motor pool jeep from another unit. It turned out I would be riding with another GI in a trailer pulled by the jeep. It had been raining, the dirt roads were slick, and the ditches were full of mud.

As we pulled out, near the front of the convoy, and turned right to head south, the trailer whipped around and then straightened up quickly when it hit the mud at the edge of the ditch, throwing out the other GI who was sitting on the left side and threw me into where he had been sitting. It

The ditch the GI was thrown into is in the foreground on the right.

looked like a scene from a "Three Stooges" movie as he went up in the air and came down in the mud still in the sitting position with his legs sticking straight out. By the time we got out of the convoy and stopped he had sunk in the mud up to his waist with his legs out of sight and was having trouble getting out. Some of the ditches are three to four feet deep. When we finally pulled him out he decided to go back, clean up, and catch another ride later.

By the time we were able to get back in the convoy we were way back toward the rear and in the middle of some "deuce-and-a half" trucks carrying troops. The convoy went smoothly; on occasions you would hear someone returning fire, until we reached the Dragon Mt. area near the 4th Division base camp, Camp Enari. We were passing slowly through a small business area, like a "strip mall," consisting of at least three dilapidated buildings in a row on one side of the street. These were wooden structures, with rusty tin and wooden roofs, with porches on the front. The businesses appeared to be of questionable intent: a bar, a strip joint, and possibly some type of clothing and trinkets outlet. They were facing the highway but on a smaller road running parallel to the one we were on and about 50 yards over. On the porch of one of the buildings were three girls, pulling their tops up and or their bottoms down and waving at the convoy. By this time, some troops had jumped off their trucks, hoping to stretch their imagination into reality, but two jeeps were driving back and forth between them and the buildings, herding them back to the convoy.

20
BASE CAMP / 1/22ND

On arriving from the Oasis I checked in at the S-1 and then escaped to take a long shower. Imagine what you might look like after riding about 20 miles in an open trailer behind a jeep at the end of a convoy on a dirt road. At the Oasis, the showers didn't always work or were sometimes out of water. I had a large wok in the XO's tent at the Oasis that I could stand in if the showers were out of water, pour water over my head from my helmet, soap down, and rinse off. The shower at base camp, 1/22nd, was two 55-gallon drums, mounted overhead up on a frame, with an emersion heater for hot water, occasionally. I think all base camp units had showers. I felt guilty sometimes because the guys in the woods were-

S-1 Headquarters Company clerks' area.

lucky if they got three showers a year, but I got over it.

I returned to the S-1 the next morning to find out which line company I was going to be assigned to. I was expecting to be sent out to one of the line companies or the Recon Platoon, which I had been originally assigned to. Instead, I was told I would be assigned to a twelve- man recon patrol that deployed around the 4th Division base camp. These usually took several days, including a briefing and debriefing. However, I would only be going on every other patrol each week.

Each patrol would usually be made up of personnel from your unit, considering the personnel available. The infantry units in 4th Division base camp provided most of the personnel for these patrols and sometimes you went out with or had personnel from other units. I was still assigned to Head Quarters Company, Recon Platoon, but never went out with them the rest of my nine plus months. Between patrols, and S-5 that came later, I occasionally flew out to a fire base, one of the line companies or the recon platoon as a forward clerk, typing requests, etc., sometimes taking pens, paper, razors, mail, metal mirrors, etc. For the rest of the time while I was

in base camp, not on patrols or S-5, I was on guard duty, ammo runs, as a guard on trucks going off base to pick up and deliver locals, and supervising the construction to convert tents on wooden frames to wooden buildings.

S-1, looking east. The tents were converted to buildings. Below: Looking west over top corner of S-1 to Dragon Mountain.

21
PICK UP AND DELIVERY

"...but blessed is he who is generous to the poor."
—Pro. 14:21

"If it is possible, as much as it depends on you, live peaceably with all men."
—Rom. 12.18

One of my first details was to ride shotgun, or in the back of a "deuce and a half," picking up and delivering locals who work inside the 4th Division base camp. A truck from 4th Division would come by the S-1 early in the morning to

pick up anyone on the detail. There was a driver with three riflemen, one riding shotgun in the cab, the others in the back, on each run.

The detail would go out the north gate in the morning, pick up the locals at their homes, all hired and previously cleared by the 4th Division, and return them in the afternoon around 4 or 5. They were allowed to bring in a small bag, usually rice for lunch, but this had to be searched coming and going.

On rare occasions, someone would try to sneak something out hidden in some food or somewhere in the bag, usually something small like a razor blade or a small battery. This would lead to them getting released; the others would find out and this would cure thievery. A lot of them would be given food during the day, almost always fruit, which we would have to inspect and then were supposed to keep. The detail sergeant had suggested if we cut the fruit up sufficiently to inspect it, we might give it back to them. From his suggestion we allowed them to keep the food on our trips and wouldn't be surprised if it happened almost all the time on the other trucks. Times were tough for civilians, especially when it came to food.

Fortunately, the truck I went on never ran over a mine or was attacked.

22
AMMO RUNS

"You ought to say, 'If it is the Lord's will, we will live and do this or that.'"
—James 4:15

Ammo runs were normally scheduled during the day when they weren't as dangerous, always with a predetermined number of tanks and other escort vehicles for the number of trucks needed. The ones I had to go on started from base camp, went to the ammo dump near Pleiku, and returned the

tank #36 of 3rd Platoon, 1/10 Cav

same way. However, sometimes after a particular busy day in the artillery section, an ammo run would have to be made at night. You never felt like you had enough escorts. The hair would stand up on your arms at the slightest unusual sound, which you could not determine because of all the noise the vehicles made. Usually you couldn't see much of anything, either, and it seemed like it was always a moonless night when we made a run.

The ammo was carried in deuce-and-a-half trucks, some with M-60 machine gun mounts on one or both corners at the front of the truck bed.

I never got to ride on one with a machine gun. You either rode shotgun in the cab or back in the bed; I am glad I never had to ride shotgun. The biggest thing to worry about was running over a mine, especially on the way back with a truck full of ammo. If you ran over a mine while riding shotgun up front in the cab, well, I just figured if I was riding back in the truck bed I might land in a soft area off the road, if the ammo didn't blow up, too. At any rate, this detail could take a big toll on your nerves.

23
RECON PATROLS

"Trust in the Lord with all your heart, and lean not on your own understanding; In all your ways acknowledge Him, and He shall direct your paths."
—*Pro. 3:5-6*

The main purpose of a recon patrol is to observe and report any enemy movement, without being observed or engaging the enemy, and if required, directing fire from other sources: artillery, mortars, Puff the Magic Dragon, or the little piper cubs (loaded with under wing rockets), and helicopters, not to leave out F4 Phantoms or WWII props.

Taking a break.

A deserted village.

An inhabited village.

We always left base camp in a deuce-and-a-half truck. The patrol area was just outside artillery range around the 4th Division base camp. We, "almost" always, started from a drop-off point just east of the road that led out the north side of camp, inside artillery range, covering the same general area on each patrol. We would call in from the drop-off point then go east moving out of artillery range to the coordinates on our "funny papers." "Funny papers" are clear papers with marks that denote our ground objectives and are also marked so we know how to place them over our maps – important.

We would continue east to a certain point then go south to a certain point then turn west to our pick-up point. This usually brought us to the south end of base camp. We would call in before we entered a village, if we observed any enemy, when we reached each objective, when we stopped for the night, and when we were getting close to the pick-up point. Also, we reported any enemy positions and any conditions that would affect the patrol so base camp would always know where we were in case we needed help.

On rare occasions, a dog team, one man and one dog, went with us. The main reason we almost always covered the same area was because the "operation center" wanted each patrol to know their area like it was their back yard. The coordinates for each patrol were always supposed to be different, but just in case we knew better than to walk on paths or go any route exactly as we had before.

The highest rank of the twelve men on these patrols was sergeant E-5, two on each patrol: One was in charge of the maps and overlays and getting us out and back, the other was in charge of the men and deployment in case we couldn't avoid contact with the enemy. On each patrol, the sergeant who was taking it out had to go to the operation center for a briefing before going out and a debriefing on returning.

As we left the drop-off point, one rifleman would start out in front, on point, followed by one rifleman on each flank; this was the widest part of the patrol. The middle of the patrol was made up of the two sergeants, two radio men, at least one medic, and three or four more riflemen, one of which trailed way behind but kept at least one person in sight. One sergeant and one radioman stayed toward the front, and the other sergeant and radioman toward the rear of the patrol. The point and flank men watched for booby traps and ambushes, the middle men provided back-up fire, the man in the rear watched for spider holes. All watched for enemy movement.

During the rainy season when the foliage was thicker, we covered an area about the size of a baseball diamond; in the dry season with little or no cover we spread out at least the size of a baseball field or bigger. When I went on my first patrol, I was assigned to "pull up the rear," looking for spider holes. Spider holes were similar to tunnel entrances, well camouflaged, but rarely connected to tunnels in our area, just holes in the ground. The VC (Vietcong) would dig these in patrolled areas then hide in them when they thought a patrol was coming. After a patrol went by, they would pop up and spray the rear of the patrol with automatic weapon fire then run away. I stayed at this position in the patrol until I made sergeant.

A (fairly) Secure Village

24
IN A TIGHT SPOT

"Stand in the ways and see, and ask for the safe paths,
where the good way is, and walk in it."
—Jer. 6:16

On the last day of one patrol as we were leaving a tree line and moving into shoulder-high grass, someone spotted some movement in the grass about 70 yards away that looked like it was moving toward us. We decided to move all the way into the grass because the ground in the tree line was higher and we didn't want to be spotted and didn't think we had been.

We crouched down, waiting and ready, hoping they would pass by without seeing us and hence avoiding a fire fight. As mentioned earlier, we were not to make contact unless it was unavoidable, report observations, call in fire support (a huey gun ship or a piper cub loaded with rockets), and if necessary direct fire and engage the enemy if ordered to.

When they were passing by about 25 yards abreast we still hadn't seen them but heard one of them talking and realized they were GIs. We couldn't say anything, because the danger was too great; they, like us, would think they were the only friendly patrol in the area. As soon as they left the area we radioed base camp, especially considering they may have reported us, but "operations" didn't know of anyone that should be that close to us. When we reached our pick-up point, our ride was waiting for us so we figured we were the ones in the right area.

On any occasion, while on these recon patrols, if we came under fire from a village or sniper, and it wasn't an ambush or fire fight, and couldn't escape safely without returning fire, we had to call in and report where we were receiving fire from, before we could return fire. If the area was designated as a friendly village or an area that could be covered by another patrol, we could not return fire, unless it was to save lives, ahem, just "de de mow," get out of the area as quickly as possible.

THE ENEMY IN YOUR HANDS

1. HANDLE HIM FIRMLY, PROMPTLY, BUT HUMANELY.

   The captive in your hands must be disarmed, searched, secured and watched. But he must also be treated at all times as a human being. He must not be tortured, killed, mutilated, or degraded, even if he refuses to talk. If the captive is a woman, treat her with all respect due her sex.

2. TAKE THE CAPTIVE QUICKLY TO SECURITY

   As soon as possible evacuate the captive to a place of safety and interrogation designated by your commander. Military documents taken from the captive are also sent to the interrogators, but the captive will keep his personal equipment except weapons.

3. MISTREATMENT OF ANY CAPTIVE IS A CRIMINAL OFFENSE. EVERY SOLDIER IS PERSONALLY RESPONSIBLE FOR THE ENEMY IN HIS HANDS.

   ... to mistreat a captive. It is also a punishable offense. Not even a beaten enemy will surrender if he knows his captors will torture or kill him. He will resist and make his capture more costly. Fair treatment of captives encourages the enemy to surrender.

4. TREAT THE SICK AND WOUNDED CAPTIVE AS BEST YOU CAN.

   The captive saved may be an intelligence source. In any case he is a human being and must be treated like one. The soldier who ignores the sick and wounded degrades his uniform.

5. ALL PERSONS IN YOUR HANDS, WHETHER SUSPECTS, CIVILIANS, OR COMBAT CAPTIVES, MUST BE PROTECTED AGAINST VIOLENCE, INSULTS, CURIOSITY, AND REPRISALS OF ANY KIND.

   Leave punishment to the courts and judges. The soldier shows his strength by his fairness, firmness, and humanity to the persons in his hands.

25
THE REAL VOLUNTEER

After several patrols, I noticed one of the medics was always on every one of our patrols. I asked one of the other patrol members about him one day and was told he always volunteered for both of the patrols each week. I don't remember the last time I saw him but did find out he had "DERO Sed," gone home, a real volunteer and a man who walked worthy of his calling.

KEY PHRASES

ENGLISH	VIETNAMESE
Halt	Đừng lại
Lay down your gun	Buông súng xuống
Put up your hands	Đưa tay lên
Keep your hands on your head	Đưa hai lên đầu
I will search you	Tôi khám ông
Do not talk	Đừng nói chuyện
Walk there	Lại đằng kia
Turn Right	Xây bên phải
Turn Left	Xây bên trái

" The courage and skill of our men in battle will be matched by their magnanimity when the battle ends. And all American military action in Vietnam will stop as soon as aggression by others is stopped."

27 August 1965   Lyndon B. Johnson

THE ENEMY IN YOUR HANDS

AS A MEMBER OF THE US MILITARY FORCES, YOU WILL COMPLY WITH THE GENEVA PRISONER OF WAR CONVENTIONS OF 1949 TO WHICH YOUR COUNTRY ADHERES. UNDER THESE CONVENTIONS :

YOU CAN AND WILL

DISARM YOUR PRISONER
IMMEDIATELY SEARCH HIM THOROUGHLY
REQUIRE HIM TO BE SILENT
SEGREGATE HIM FROM OTHER PRISONERS
GUARD HIM CAREFULLY
TAKE HIM TO THE PLACE DESIGNATED BY YOUR COMMANDER

YOU CANNOT AND MUST NOT

MISTREAT YOUR PRISONER
HUMILIATE OR DEGRADE HIM
TAKE ANY OF HIS PERSONAL EFFECTS WHICH DO NOT HAVE SIGNIFICANT MILITARY VALUE
REFUSE HIM MEDICAL TREATMENT IF REQUIRED AND AVAILABLE

ALWAYS TREAT YOUR PRISONER HUMANELY

26
THE LOST PATROL

We left through the "north" gate as usual and radioed from the drop-off point that we were headed east. We had a staff sergeant (E-6) taking us out who was not from our unit and someone I had never met before. When we reached our coordinates for the night, he said he had radioed in each time during the day when we reached a point on the overlay but felt like we were not in the right place, and we weren't sure we were at the right spot now. I didn't see him put the map and overlays together. He said he was going to call in and have a flare fired as soon as it got dark so we could check our position. We were out of range, but should have been able to see a flare.

After having flares fired three times and not seeing anything, I asked if I could look at the map. He took out the overlay and placed it over the map. I looked at it for a few seconds and realized the overlay was upside down. He said he looked at the map before we left but was familiar with the area so I guess he was just casually looking at the "funny paper." He said he told the driver to take us to the usual drop-off point, which was out the "north" gate. According to the overlay, we were supposed to go out the "south" gate and go east. I had never been on a patrol that went out the south gate. He then asked for a flare to be shot to the northeast section which we saw and were able to determine our position and advise base. They gave us coordinates for the next day to get picked up and said they would notify the other patrol in the area. I'm sure glad that I didn't have to go to that debriefing.

27
EXPERIENCE IS A GOOD TEACHER

"Therefore you also be ready, for the Son of Man is coming
at an hour you do not expect."
—James 1:5

While watching the guys load onto the back of our truck to head out on another patrol, I noticed the last two to get on board were carrying an M-60 machine gun and ammo box. We were running late from waiting for everyone to show up so I didn't say anything at the time. We should have already made our first radio check at the drop-off point. Radio checks were important because they are how base camp kept up with the patrols. From experience they knew approximately how long it took for a patrol to get from one point to another. If something happened, they could start looking for us from the last checkpoint.

In route I asked them why they had brought a machine gun, and they said it was what they wanted to carry. I didn't ask them who told them they could bring it or even how they got it; had they asked me I would have given them a break and said, "No, you're not taking it." Maybe it was to see if I would send them back but we were running late and they were going with us. Anyway, they carried it, one the gun and one the ammo, all day switching around. At night after we had split into two groups about 25 yards apart, I heard a lot of metal clanging coming from the other group. We always split into two groups, each one with a sergeant, radioman, and a medic in case we are attacked and overrun so hopefully one group can get out a radio call for help. Also, we had just finished moving about 50 yards and I didn't want to have to move again after dark. When you are in an area of suspected enemy movement, you pick a spot to set up just at dusk but look for another place to move to quickly and "quietly" after dark in case you had been spotted. Twelve guys out in the middle of nowhere don't need any surprises in the middle of the night, right?

I went over to where these two with the machine gun had set up and I asked them what they were doing and told them to keep it quiet. They said they were trying to load it. I told them they were not to fire it if they did get it loaded unless their location was being overrun. A machine gun draws more fire than any other weapon on a battlefield and is a favorite target for a sniper. I suggested they first throw hand grenades; it's hard to tell where they come from, especially at night, then after the rest of us escape in the confusion, they could fire away and then try to catch up with us when they can. Well, needless to say they were not happy campers, having to carry that load for three days without many prospects of using it.

28
A TIGHTER SPOT

"Commit your way to the Lord; trust in him."
—Psalm 37:5

"Behold, how good and how pleasant it is for brothers to dwell together in unity!"
—Psalm 133:1

On another patrol, we received a radio call to check on a village nearby where some activity had been reported. We left the area we were in and turned east toward the village which sat on a slight hill. We continued east through a rice paddy then up a draw toward the front of the village. About halfway up the draw we split, leaving half the patrol to cover us if we had to make a hasty retreat. The rest of us continued crawling until we reached a point where we were looking north, directly up the road that went into the village. The foliage was thick enough that we felt we had not been seen.

The road came out of the village about 50 yards toward us then turned left about twenty yards in front of us and went around in a half circle to our east until it was behind us then straightened out about 40 yards behind us heading south again. We had been watching the village for about 15 minutes, not seeing anything, when we heard some motor vehicles coming up the road from the south behind us. These turned out to be ARVNs, South VN troops, with several vehicles that looked like small tanks with big rubber tires; I think they were called "Vs."

Just as the ARVNs reached a point in the road that put us directly between them and the village, a firefight broke out from the village with the ARVNs. We were right in the middle but evidently neither knew we were there. We immediately started crawling back down the draw with our radioman calling our other group to tell them it was us coming down and for them to call for air support, usually a Huey gunship, to help us all get out of there. Once we caught up with the rest of our group we radioed again advising we were not receiving fire and that we would be moving west with the lead man and the rear man waving poncho liners so we could be recognized by the Huey. The Huey gun ship had arrived to cover our escape but held back at a safe distance since we were not receiving direct fire from anyone as we "dee dee mowed" (moved very quickly) from the area. We were extremely fortunate not to lose anyone and learned a good lesson about not leaving our rear open to chance circumstances.

29
DON'T DROP YOUR "GUARD"

One morning in base camp while visiting one of our two "three holers" I noticed the "deuce-and-a-half" latrine duty truck was backing up faster than usual. At the last second I sprang through the latrine door, my pants around my ankles, as the truck backed into the side of it and pushed it off into the drainage ditch beside the road, just missing the other latrine. The driver said he misjudged the distance and then his foot slipped off the brake pedal.

The next day, when I went back for a return visit, I noticed the latrine duty man, not the same one, had already

The outhouses are the white buildings on the right side of the road.

unloaded some boards and was now going to pull the cans from the other "three-holer," the one I was in. I asked him to leave one can under me and he did. The usual procedure was to remove the cans, pour kerosene in them and burn off the contents. Then these cans are dumped into bins on the back of the truck and taken out to the dump for further burning.

I watched him empty the kerosene container into the two cans he had pulled out then walk around to the other side of the truck. He came back with another container and poured more into the two latrine cans. He then went back to the cab of the truck and returned with some matches. I decided it was time to leave because I didn't want to sit there smelling those cans burn. When he lit the match and threw it in one of the cans the whole area went "whoosh" and was up in flames. I jumped out again holding my pants up with my hands.

What he didn't think about was those cans are full of holes.

What I didn't know was he had run out of kerosene and had poured gas into those cans, which ran out all over the area.

Another latrine bit the dust. I don't remember how the fire was finally put out or what the excuse was this time. I do remember giving some thought about how the woods might be safer and also as to what my dad would have thought about my demise had I been "wasted" in the latrine.

30
S - 5

Sometime in early June, I asked to be assigned to S-5, (Civil Affairs and Medical Evacuation) in addition to the recon patrols. Not really volunteering, but an exchange from supervising the conversion of "wibetops" (probably not correct spelling but that's what it sounded like), tents with wooden frames, to all wooden buildings, and hopefully getting off those nerve-racking ammo runs. However, I was told that at the time they didn't need anyone.

The S-5 often provided security for the medical personnel when they went out to treat locals and helped move villages, usually "Montengards" (indigenous people in Vietnam, and usually an ally of the U.S.). which were in this part of

the country, to areas that could be reasonably secured by ARVN troops, and sometimes ours. Their houses, which set up on stilts or poles like beach houses, were moved on top of

deuce-and-a-half trucks and trailers while they moved their personal belongings in ox carts, herding their animals while everything was being moved.

The S-5 also went out in a three-vehicle detail to treat locals, again mostly "Montengards," for whatever medical attention they needed, from gunshot and shrapnel wounds to the plague shots. The lead jeep, equipped with a .50-caliber machine gun, was usually manned by an officer, rifleman, and machine gunner. The second vehicle was a deuce-and-a-half, carrying a battalion

Captain Castillio is in the center.

surgeon, some medics, medical supplies, and a rifleman. The third vehicle, a jeep ambulance, carried a driver and a rifleman. They only stayed out from morning until afternoon, with other fire support available and within artillery range. When they pulled into a village with the medical detail the people and their children would line up behind the truck like they were waiting to see the family doctor. Sometimes someone would be a little apprehensive, usually because they were suffering from a shrapnel or bullet wound.

Montengards almost always received these wounds from Vietcong or NVAs. I wished everyone back home could have seen just one of these visits or one village being moved to realize how much good human relations were accomplished by the S-5 every time they went into a village. They were always welcomed in these villages.

In July '67, the patrol was ambushed by VC, Capt. Castillio was killed, and machine gunner Rice was wounded riding in the lead jeep. I was then assigned to take Rice's position and alternated between S-5 and the recon platoon until the end of my tour. A little later, I also became security for Lt. Skirchak when he went on pay call outside the base camp.

31
MONEY MATTERS

Lt. Skirchak had recently become the Headquarters XO and the battalion pay officer. He had spent his first six months with one of our line companies and would finish up his tour at this new position. I had heard that those who served with him said he was the best and was the most-liked field officer we had. I heard he was a good shot, too, coming within a few yards of hitting his target with a M-79 grenade launcher at its maximum range, a few hundred yards. I think he was nineteen.

I had stopped in the S-1 for something, don't remember what, and was talking with the S-1 clerk. Both of us could

Lt. Skirchak.

hear the CO and XO talking because they had left their door open. We were not listening to them, but both of us heard it when one of them referred to me. We caught the part that said "Sgt. Graves." I was thinking about making a quick exit when the CO called out to the clerk to send for Sgt. Graves.

When I went in he told me that Lt. Skirchak had asked for me. This is when I met Lt. Skirchak and learned of my new latest duty as his security or guard if he had to leave base camp on pay call. Almost everyone out in the field had made arrangements on their pay but there was always someone who wanted some cash. We went on these pay calls whenever Lt. Skirchak could get us a ride, almost always in a Huey.

As time went by, we became good friends, (as good as a commissioned officer and non-commissioned officers could be). I never did learn why he had asked for me to be his security.

On top of The Hill / Lt. Skirchak on far rt

32
THE HILL

In addition to pay call, I also went with Lt. Skirchak on guard duty to a hill that overlooked a lake that was one of the base camp's water supplies. On one occasion when coming down the hill, the transmission popped out of gear. The driver could not get it back in gear and the hill was so steep the brakes on that dirt road were useless, so we came down free-wheeling it. Once we got down on level ground the driver got it stopped. Then everyone wanted to do it again, almost everyone, and see how fast we were going. I said, we should have a picture of this, and being the only one with a camera, I said I'd get out and take pictures as they came down again. Boys will be boys; anyway, everyone survived.

33
THE PLEIKU EXPRESS

Between recon and S-5, and if I wasn't going somewhere with Lt. Skirchak, Chuck, an E-5 from the motor pool, and I would try to find some reason to go to town, Pleiku. Chuck was always checking with the COMMO shop, S-4, supply, or the aid station and I with the S-1 to see if anyone needed anything from anywhere around base camp. Chuck could

always get a jeep to go anywhere around base camp to pick up stuff but you always needed a reason and an officer to go off base.

Sgt. Chuck.

Once everyone learned we would go by Pleiku, either coming or going, to get whatever we were after, people started thinking of things to go after. At first we always had to have an officer with us to leave base camp – some of them went to get away also – but after a while (I guess they decided we'd come back anyway), if none of them could get away, we would get a pass to go off base without an officer. The first trip started out with the COMMO officer then other officers and eventually Lt. Skirchak found out about our trips and he started going with us whether he needed anything or not.

Sometimes an officer would want to be dropped off at a club or somewhere and picked up when we were on our way back, but Lt. Skirchak liked to ride to town with us no matter what the reason. It was only fair that Chuck and I took turns driving, because whenever we stopped in town, one of us, I or Chuck, had to stay with the jeep. Jeeps had a way of disappearing if left alone. When we first started these trips I would drive because Chuck said he had done enough driving around the motor pool.

One day when I was driving and noticed in the mirror that Lt. Skirchak wasn't wearing his bars, I said to Chuck, "Should a sergeant be driving or should a private be driving?"

Chuck said, "I don't know but the LT told me once before he didn't mind driving, but I don't want to get in trouble with someone driving this jeep without a license so go on driving."

I looked back in the mirror and Lt. Skirchak was grinning, I don't know if it was because he felt like one of the guys (which he was) even though he was in charge or he was just having a good day. The chain of command works best when everyone understands why and how it works and respects everyone accordingly. He was a real "all right" personable officer.

34
NHA TRANG

"Greater love has no one than this, that one lay down his life for his friends."
—John 15:13

"For this reason you be ready too; for the Son of Man is coming at an hour when you do not think He will."
—Matt 24:44

Lt. Skirchak asked me one day if I had known a certain lieutenant, I don't remember his name now. I told him I had seen him in base camp before I went to the Oasis. He was surprised because he said he had been looking everywhere for someone who knew him or what he looked like but

hadn't found anyone. He told me the lieutenant had been on TDY (temporary duty) down south of Ban Me Thuot with some ARVNs for months. II CORPS had advised 1/22nd that he had been killed and his body sent to Nha Trang. They needed someone who had seen him to identify the body. Lt. Skirchak said it looked like we'd have to go down there.

We got there late in the day and a jeep met us at the air base. The driver said he would drop me off first where I'd stay the night and then take Lt. Skirchak to the officer's quarters. When we got to where I was supposed to stay, the end of the building had been blown up with a satchel charge earlier and everyone alive had been moved to another building and they were now out of space unless I would stay in the other end of the blown-up building. I rode with them to the officer's quarters, a real nice two- story house with marble floors, but I didn't get to stay there, either.

The next day we went to what must have been a morgue where the lieutenant was brought out in a body bag. It was unzipped so we could see his face, I said that was him, and then signed something. We then headed back to Camp Enari.

Flying High

35
FLYING HIGH & LOW

The routine for coming and going in helicopters between two bases was always going out high or low and returning high or low depending on how you left the first one; this obviously, is to avoid collisions.

I had caught a ride on a Huey carrying supplies out to one of the line companies and we were going out low. I was sitting on the floor with my back to crates stacked in the middle of the chopper, higher than my head. My legs were crossed with my knees sticking out a little past the edge of the floor. We were just over the tree tops "zig zagging" a little and following the lay of the land, occasionally flying over a river bed.

All of a sudden there was a big bang followed by a spray of water coming through the prop wash. The next thing that happened was we veered left then turned hard right and then hard left and then hard right again, getting out of the area quickly. I was sitting on the right side. When we were in the high bank of the first right turn, after veering left a little,

I was leaning over and looked between my legs. Normally this would be looking down toward the ground, but I could see the sky with the trees upside down between my knees now and the ground was directly in

front of me when I looked straight out the door opening, then nothing but sky when we banked high on the next left turn, followed with the trees upside down again and with the sky above them, on the second high bank to the right. I never did hear what we had flown over, but one thing for sure, I never got on a ride like that at the county fair.

When I was getting strapped in to make my first flight riding shotgun on the outside of a Huey and the pilot learned it was my first trip, he made sure I was aware of the circumstances that could arise. He told me that, "on the average,"

Riding shotgun.

when receiving ground fire, you (me) would have about seven seconds (on the average) to find the source of the ground fire, return fire, and stop the ground fire before it zeroed in on us. (But who's counting?)

72

36
PAY DAY KONTUM

On regular pay days, Lt. Skirchak could be carrying as much as 40,000 in MPCs (military pay currency); however, I don't think he carried anywhere near that much when we left base camp to go out to where one of the line companies was. Usually he would tell me a little in advance when we were going on a pay call. Sometimes when he was having trouble getting a ride he would just send word for me to meet him at the S-1 and wait. It happened like this one day when we were going to Kontum.

I was on my way to the S-1 when he got the call that we

"The Unknown Soldier" (Lt. Skirchak).

had a ride. I only had three M-16 magazines with me – 60 rounds – all we could carry around in base camp at that time because of an accident in base camp with someone getting wounded. (This didn't last long and we soon went back to carrying whatever amount of ammo we wanted to carry.)

When I got to the S-1 I said I was going to go pick up some more ammo.

He said, "We don't have time, we can get more ammo when we get where we are going."

When I went on patrol, but not around base camp, I carried several hundred rounds of M-16 ammo, two bandoleers with eight magazines in each bandoleer, 20 rounds each mag, a large and a small ammo pouch on my belt, at least 12 more mags, and two or three magazines taped together in my M-16. I also carried two "willie pee" (white phosphorus) and two "frag" (fragment) grenades, Bill Jones' knife and a picture of my hero Gabby Hayes.

Some of the guys used to kid me about my ammo – until I made sergeant – but I always remembered what someone said, "It's better to have it and not need it then to need it and not have it." You felt … kinda naked … with just three magazines.

Anyway, we caught our ride, but as we were approaching Kontum the pilot told Lt. Skichak it was under attack from the northwest section and may be overrun. He asked us if we wanted to get out. Lt. Skirchak asked him to check and see if anyone was waiting at the chopper pad to pick us up, and where was the pad in reference to our troops. The pilot said the pad was in the northeast section, there was a river that came down the west side of town then turned east across the south end of town and then went south again. There was a bridge across the river in the southwest section to where our troops were located, oh, and also there was someone waiting for us with a jeep.

Lt. Skirchak said, "Put us down. He will probably need help getting back across the bridge."

I reminded him we, I, only had five magazines between us, plus his .45. We got two more magazines off the chopper. The pilot said he wasn't going to land, just come in quick and hover long enough for us to jump and run. Well, I did have my movie camera in my large ammo pouch at this time so I took it out and got a bunch of pictures as we flew into the chopper pad at Kontum. Lt. Skirchak was shaking his head and gritting his teeth when we jumped out and ran for the

Tanks headed north to bridge to Kontum.

jeep but he never said a word about me taking pictures.

The only person left at the pad was our driver; everyone else was just pulling out. I don't believe we ever had more than one wheel on the ground all the way to the bridge. We didn't see a soul until we crossed the bridge, and these were GIs. The first thing we passed on the other side of the bridge was part of the artillery battery with all guns pointed toward town, 105s, 155s, and 175s, and some infantry with a re-coil-less rifle on a jeep. To my knowledge, no one fired on our base the rest of the day or that night and I never did hear what happened in Kontum.

The next day, Lt. Skirchak had pay call, during which someone put down their M-16 and picked up his. He didn't notice it until we were getting on a Huey to go back. He handed me the weapon, took mine, and told me to catch a ride back when I found his, because he wasn't going back to base camp with someone else's weapon (ahem?). I went to the COMMO shop and got them to call our S-4, gave them the serial number on the weapon and found out who it be-longed to. I also found out that there was a convoy leaving for the base camp in two days and I could ride back in it. I got the weapons switched and "borrowed" enough ammo to make me feel better.

37
BAN ME THUOT FAST FOOD

"The Lord is good to all;
He has compassion on all He has made."
—Psalms 145:9

Ban Me Thuot was "in country" R&R for ARVNs. 1/22nd had a few troops down here on TDY; I always wondered what they were doing there.

Anyway, after pay call, Lt. Skirchak went to the officer's mess and I went to the ARVN's mess area and found a GI's mess area also. The ARVN and GI mess areas were located in two wooden buildings which were side by side, the same size (approximately 30 by 80 feet), a porch on each at the same end, and not enough space between the buildings to walk between them.

Ours seemed to be a general purpose building, etc., with the mess area on the porch, consisting of an emersion heater in a 55-gallon drum heating C rations. Next door was the ARVN's "recreational" facility, with a mess area on its porch, consisting of one very large wok. They sure had some pretty girls come and go from their recreational building; however, GIs weren't allowed in.

Oh, well, I grabbed a C ration and was just about to drop it in the hot water drum when I noticed several GIs trading their rations for whatever was in the wok next door. I decided to try it; it looked like it was mostly rice with what could have been chives, or something green, and some little brown things I took for some kind of root vegetable. I handed over my rations, my mess kit got filled up, and I sat down on the porch to eat with a couple of other GIs. I looked out at the perimeter which started about 50 yards out. In this area there was a maze of trenches with grass-covered mounds in front, about 2 feet high, about 20 to 30 yards deep and about 100 yards wide. It looked like it had been an old fortification. I imagine if you were approaching from the other side you wouldn't know the trenches were there.

At some point, I looked down at the rice and realized the little brown things were moving. I asked one of the guys sitting there what these were, he told me to look over at the grass paddies where some locals were digging in the bank. He said they were some kind of grub, he thought, that they were digging out of the bank. The other guy said they were a "delacontessions" (this spelling is how I remember he pronounced it).

"Dele what?" I said.

He said it again so I just let it go.

They looked like the "roly poly" bugs we had back home, only a little bigger, brown instead of grey, but they didn't roll up when you tried to pick them up. He said I'd probably already eaten a bunch of them. I decided to continue but didn't look. I didn't get far before I decided to see how many were left. I dug around in my kit and found a lot more on the bottom, probably trying to keep from being eaten. I decided they had been successful and turned them loose.

38
NEWS FROM HOME

Letters from home were the mainstay of hope and the assurance that life went on in the places we remembered. I received many more letters from my wife and family then I sent and appreciated and cherished them.

We had our chaplains and Bibles, or New Testaments from the Gideons to fall back on when we needed them and these were a tremendous help, but they were here and our letters came from home. The letters were our connection to what was waiting for us. Mail, local newspapers, the Stars & Stripes were all welcome but sometimes could be a small source of anxiety, especially when we read about some of the things that were going on back home. When my mail caught up with me at 1/22nd I'd been "in country" a little while.

In a letter from home I learned that Gary Anthony, "in country" about six weeks before me, had been wounded in late March or early April. Gary was with the 1st Battalion, 2nd Brigade, of the 25th Infantry (Tropical Lightening). He was one of my best friends, the second friend I made when we moved to Hickory at the start of the eighth grade. He was a PC driver on an operation that had taken his unit into an area known for mine fields. He had stood up to drive, this put his head through the terrot, which normally was above him while sitting to drive, when he ran over a mine. Standing up probably saved his life. He was blown out of the PC through the terrot, suffering shoulder and knee injuries and a broken foot.

In another letter from home in June I learned Gary had been sent home because his younger sister had drowned in a high school graduation swimming party.

In November, in another letter from home, I learned that Landis had been wounded and was in the 71st Medevac Hospital in the 4th Division base camp. He had been brought there Nov. 12 when he was wounded at Dak To. I got over there for an afternoon and discovered that none of his injuries were life threatening. We swapped some stories to catch up; he said he was with A Company 1/8th. They started out in the Ia Drang Valley in late April, then they went to a Special Forces camp at Duc Co for the start of "Nine Days in May Battle," that started on the 18th and lasted until the 26th. They found the Lost Platoon of B Company, 1/8 Infantry, 4th Inf. Div., that had lost approximately 25 of approximately 30 men, on May 19.

The combined losses of companies, A, B, and C of 1/8th during this operation, were 48 KIAs. He said he had been on other operations leading up to Dak To but this was probably the worst and it was here that he got wounded. He was expecting to get sent back to his unit in a day or two. It was tough hearing about others, here and at home, and not being able to follow up on how they were doing.

My dad, knowing the "trading" value of some items as a "one time" supply sergeant, would send me a pint of fresh brewed, right out of the western N.C. mountains, "white lightening," about once a month, after I reached the 1/22nd. It came in a plastic bottle in a cardboard box well packed. He would always send a note in advance to tell me it was on the way so I could look out for it and advise him if I didn't get it. However, every time it got through unbroken and not leaking. I usually shared this with those who met in the base camp supply room in the evening.

P.S.: Sometimes the mess sergeant would bring something to cook "in" the supply room on a gas grill the supply sergeant had. We would never have gotten away with this outside. Once we had water buffalo steaks. One of the line companies had "accidently" killed one that belonged to a village; it had to be replaced. I don't remember how the mess sergeant wound up with part of the one that was killed. A little cook-in with some of the guys, plus cakes and cookies and "other stuff" we had received from home, and anywhere else, made the day.

The supply room.

39
WHAT? NO ICE

On the second day of a recon patrol, we had stopped to take a break on the side of a hill that sloped gradually down toward a rice paddy. There were several locals working in the paddy about 300 yards away. The guys on the low side of the hill were keeping an eye on them when they noticed someone else was walking toward us. We got ready to move quickly in case he was giving directions to the enemy on our position by "walking us in." The guys down hill told him to stop when he got about 50 yards away.

He was carrying a large brown bag which he put down

"Yei, you buy coke!"

when he stopped. He then opened the bag and took out what looked like a bottle and yelled "Yei (GI) you buy coke!"

Some of the guys went down to check him and his bag out and then brought him up to us. Here was a kid out in the middle of nowhere with a bag full of 16 oz. Coca-Colas. No telling where he got them but he was headed somewhere to sell them, saw us and decided to try us first. According to those who bought one they were good, but hot.

P.S.: All the bottle caps were Coke bottle caps.

40
COVERED

One of my first patrols took us into a deserted village. All the buildings were gone but it hadn't been long since someone had been there. This looked like something S-5 would

do, move a village to a more secure area. Usually villages don't get moved unless the area has become very dangerous.

Suspecting this, we spread out more than normal to walk through the village and continue the patrol. It was a little more than approximately 50 yards square. Coming from my position in the rear as we entered the village I fell in on the right in the second row close to the edge of the village. About halfway through I came up on an area that looked like it had been a corral with a lot of the fencing missing. By the time I got through it I knew I'd been through a corral. I looked like I'd been peppered, I was covered with so many fleas.

Later that day when we passed a canal I thought about pulling a Brer Fox by jumping in and slowly sinking up to my nose to force the fleas to climb up and hopefully jump off. I did jump in but quickly got out, hoping I got rid of some of them. I knew that when I got out I had to make a quick check for leeches, trying to get rid of one bug could lead to another. A good de-fleaing back in base camp would take care of the rest (until the next time).

'I hope this wasn't a corral'

41
DOS AND DON'TS

"If any of you lacks wisdom, let him ask of God, who gives to all liberally and without reproach, and it will be given to him." —James 1:5

On another early patrol, while we were riding out to the drop-off point, the sergeant who was taking us out gave us a lot of dos and don'ts to consider for patrols.

Dos: Get your shots, take your pills, stay as clean as possible, carry something you can use as a marker (in addition to smoke, like a poncho liner, toilet paper, etc.), sleep when you can, use unscented issued bug repellent (?), watch your step (stay out of corrals), stay off paths or trails, and close one eye while firing at night.

Don'ts: Smoke, even the day before, don't shave, even the day before, don't use scented repellent, or anything that would give your position away by smell or any other way, and don't carry anything you don't need.

I'm sure there were other suggestions I don't remember now but the point is "don't" ignore the voice of experience.

42
DWELL IN UNITY

"Behold how good and how pleasant it is for brethren to dwell in unity."
—Psalms 133:1

Coming off a patrol, I stopped in the S-1 to check in. A deuce-and-a-half was out front and two GIs were unloading boxes from it and stacking them against the back wall in the S-1. They were about one foot square and there must have been a hundred of them so far.

I asked Melvin, the S-1 clerk, what they were and he said they were "casualty feeder forms." (These were forms with a copper wire attached that you could wrap around a finger or something, that you filled out with any information on any wounded and KIAs you came on.)

There was an error made in ordering: 200 cases were ordered instead of 200 forms. He said a clerk from the 4th Division HQ had called and said they were having an IG inspection and they had more of these forms than they were supposed to and were sending over these extras and a few other items until after the inspection. I noticed two days later the forms were gone.

43
AN KHE

"Greater love has no one than this, that one lay down his life for his friends."
—John 15:13

We arrived at An Khe for pay day the day after the fire base had come under a heavy ground attack. It was so heavy they had to pitch their 105 howitzers to fire horizontally, directly into the assaults, using bee hive rounds (these were rounds similar to a shotgun shell only full of barbs instead of shot). Most of the foliage looked like it had been mowed off from about two feet up. Lt. Skirchak told me after pay call he had learned the fire base had lost one man; he had been hit while he was exposed directing the artillery fire.

44
OUT WITH THE TROOPS

One of my early flights out to a line company, as the forward clerk from base camp, I was to take requests from the troops, like pay changes, requests for transfers, etc. I was also carrying toothbrushes, paste, combs, metal mirrors, pencils, paper, hand soap, razors, Stars & Stripes, and mail. Hot food in large containers was also on the Huey. I was told this would be a fast-moving operation: land, set up, feed the troops, load up, and get out. The troops knew it was coming and that they would be rushed through the chow line, but hot food was worth it and they didn't get it often.

Fire base.

Unfortunately, when opening one of the food containers it was found to have a loose rubber seal which disclosed a condition under it that prevented it from being used: maggots.

More than likely the food had not been contaminated but that chance could not be taken. As it turned out, there was plenty to go around. Everyone got fed, then the cooks loaded up and left. I helped serve so I didn't get to see everyone who wanted to see me. A supply chopper was due the next day so I decided to stay over. That night I was placed with some guys who were to pull the second watch. Little did I know we were going to be up all night.

Part of an ARVN unit was also sent over to help on guard duty in our area. We were told a large enemy contingent had been spotted moving much faster than previously reported and would be moving through our area tonight instead of in two days. When the ARVNs that were sent over for guard duty moved in I noticed a lot of them were women, an interesting situation but from what I had heard they were quite

capable soldiers. Some of us were told to grab a quick nap.

Sometime later, someone woke me up and said they were waking everyone up, and to be quiet and stay alert. After what seemed like an hour, one of the guys whispered the enemy was moving by some as close as 50 yards, going from our left to right. There wasn't a moon out so I couldn't see anything. Next he pointed then held a scope (Starlight) up in front of my eyes for a few seconds. I noticed he didn't let go of it: You would be in a world of "you know what" if you lost one of these.

"Sure 'nuff" I couldn't count how many I saw go by. Later he said he had never seen that much enemy movement at night. The night went by without a shot being fired. The next day around noon I caught a ride back with a supply Huey.

45
THE REFRIGERATOR

One day when I had stopped in the S-1 front office, where the HQ's company clerk worked, one of the other clerks, from the back office where the line company clerks worked, asked me if I wanted to buy into their refrigerator. One of the clerks was going home and wanted to sell his share for $10. So I went back to look at it. It was small about 4 feet high, and there were ten owners, each could keep about a six pack cold, usually Nehis. I bought in.

Months later, maybe returning from Kontum but somewhere, filthy from riding in a jeep in a convoy, I went to the S-1 to check in and then to the back office to get a cold Nehi, before heading to the shower (or the 4th Division steam bath, shower, and massage that is mentioned later).

While I was standing there drinking it and jawing with

the clerks, an officer came in I had never seen before. He went over to the refrigerator, got out a drink, then asked me who I was and what I was doing in the S-1 looking like I did and where did I get that drink.

I came to attention when he addressed me and I told him who, and what, and out of "my refrigerator" sir; he now knew that I knew he couldn't have been in on it. I could tell from his next few words he didn't like the way I answered, then he told me not to come back in there again looking like I did, and then he left. I remember getting a few "thumbs up" from the clerks behind him.

One of the clerks said he was a platoon leader from one of the line companies and was always coming in and helping himself to drinks without asking or paying for them. He was recovering from something and they hoped he got well soon and would go back to where he came from. I decided to leave in case he came back. When I went out the door he was standing at one of the relief canisters set just outside the S-1 for the clerks to use while one of the "three holers" was out of order. There was an open circle of cloth on stakes that overlapped a little around this area to give you cover between your waist and knees. When he left the S-1 he was carrying a folder which was now between his teeth while his hands were being used to relieve himself. I gave him a snappy salute and "afternoon sir" as I quickly went by while he grumbled something through his teeth while attempting a salute.

In two steps I was in the supply building, then
through it, through the aid station, and out the back door, fortunately never to see him again.

46
SNOOPY

On one occasion, I rode back to base camp in a Huey with surveillance equipment that the operator called "Snoopy." It sat in the middle of the floor of the Huey toward the front of the cargo area, about a foot and a half to two feet wide, several feet long and maybe a foot and a half high. There was a screen about the size of a large dinner plate with a light pale green face on top toward the front. It sloped at about 30 degrees from front to back. (Several years ago I saw something that looked like that screen in the Batmobile in a Batman movie.)

He turned it on and little blips and marks moved from top to bottom (front to back) as we flew along. The operator said he could tell if we were passing over men or animals; it took a well-trained eye because I couldn't tell any difference even when he pointed them out.

47
FIRE WATCH

Guard duty is also fire watch in your company area. A lot of the time you can go on recon patrol or S-5 without your helmet but not on guard duty in the base camp company area. During the rainy season it can rain so hard that it gets ankle deep in just a few minutes. When it rains like that and with the water running off the roofs of the building the ditches around the buildings fill up faster than it can run off to the drainage ditches out at the street. One night, on one of my earlier times on guard duty, it was raining like this.

When making your rounds at night all the lights that can be seen from the outside or the perimeter are supposed to be turned off. A light was on in one of the buildings below the mess hall. When I got there I tried to look inside to see if anyone was in but with it raining so hard and with the water running off the roof and my helmet I couldn't see well enough. I knocked but no one answered so I stepped to the side of the stoop to open the door to reach inside and turn off the light. I was also trying to stay out of the rain as much as possible. When I did this I slipped then slid into the drainage ditch that started on each side of the stoop and then went around the building. I managed to keep my balance and wound up with my back to the building, knee deep in the water in the ditch.

About this time someone said, "What are you doing, troop?"

I just couldn't help myself: When something pops in your mind you just gat'ta say it.

"I'm looking for a fire, Sarge."

I couldn't see who it was, it was still pouring, but since there were two people, I figured it was the "sergeant of the guard" and hopefully my replacement. He told me not to get smart in front of an officer and to get on with my patrol. He didn't even offer me a hand as they turned to leave, and that's when I noticed their umbrella in the light that was still on.

48
USO SHOW

During the holidays, around Thanksgiving or Christmas, the USO put on a show at the 4th Division base camp. I put on my best shirt, borrowed a ball cap from one of the clerks with a 4th Division insignia pinned on it, grabbed my camera, and went to the show.

Certain units were scheduled to go at certain times and you had to have a pass to get into the seating area. I walked around to the back of the stage and started taking pictures of everyone back there. Jonathan Winters was also back there, taking pictures and talking with two officers.

I asked if I could get a couple of pictures for the guys back in the office who couldn't get off. He said sure then asked me to hold still while he took a picture of me. He then wanted to know where I was from, how I was doing, and some other things I don't remember now but he was taking interest in what I was doing, a nice guy.

I then walked around taking pictures from the side of the stage and out front until the show was over. Not once did anyone else question my being there.

49
RED RAIN

*"And in the shadow of Your wings I will make my refuge,
until these calamities have passed by   He shall send from
heaven and save me; He reproaches the one who would
swallow me up."*
—Psalms 57:1, 3

In the months leading up to the TET offensive, guard duty picked up considerably. TET's official date to start was Jan. 30, 1968. Everyone available was pulling guard duty and I expect all bunkers were manned to the max when possible. The base camp was getting hit almost every day somewhere with probes, ground attacks, rocket attacks, sappers, or even snipers. If you were put on guard duty outside your company area you were picked up at your S-1 and taken to your post or bunker.

One night I was placed at a bunker on the edge of one of the chopper pads between the pad and the perimeter on the east side of base camp, I think it was just above 1/22nd. The bunkers were small, only one person per bunker, sandbagged on the perimeter and north side with, to the best of my memory, a triangular-shaped roof that was also sandbagged, and only high enough to crouch under for protection from mortar air bursts. The other sides were open.

Our objective was to stop sappers from getting to the helicopters, or anyone else, who got past the perimeter bunkers in front of us; we were not to fire otherwise. It was just getting dark when we were placed and I could see the other pad bunkers north and south of me about 30 to 40 yards apart.

At one point during the night, the ground attack on our side was fierce. An AC 47, "Puff the Magic Dragon" we call him, a two-engine cargo plane with three mini- guns all mounted on one side, and two Huey gunships made at least three trips to our area to lay down fire on the perimeter. I suspect they only left to reload at the rate they were firing. "Puff" flew directly over us each time, unloading into the perimeter as it slowly swept by. The red tracers from "Puff" made it look like it was red rain.

Occasionally, some green tracers would go up but this would only draw extra fire from the Huey gunships that concentrated on small areas. The next day, when some of us were talking about the night before, one of the guys said he had heard that a mini gun, theoretically, could put a bullet in each square foot of a football field in seven to eight seconds. To me, under these circumstances, this kind of eliminates any idea the enemy might have had about having a home-field advantage.

50
GOT 'CHA COVERED

"I can do everything through Him who gives me strength."
—Phil. 4:13

On another occasion during TET, I was placed in a bunker on the north side of base camp just a little east of the main road. This bunker was bigger and much thicker than any I had manned before, easily holding three people; however, no one else was brought out at all that night. All the bunkers in this area were this size.

I was told not to fire until someone got through the perimeter wire and that I would have plenty of backup. A large-scale ground attack was expected during the night. I noticed a quad 50 (four .50 caliber machine guns mounted to fire together), was on the back of a deuce-and-a-half, moving behind my bunker. The sergeant who placed me there said there was one of these quad 50s for every three bunkers. He was also the one who told me he would be bringing two more people to the bunker I was in.

Several ground attacks were tried in this area during the night. Automatic weapon fire was heavy on several occasions. During these times I could hear bullets whizzing by or striking the sand bags. However, not once did anyone get past the perimeter. During one of these attacks I took a picture of the perimeter. I rarely took my camera on guard duty but this time I had it with me. Being by myself, I kept moving from one side of the bunker to the other, keeping below the opening facing the perimeter as I went from side to side so I could keep up with the whole area in front of the bunker. I felt like there was too much flying around to expose myself in the middle of the opening or anymore than what it took to look out from one side and then the other to cover the perimeter. On one occasion while going from one side to the other I took out my camera and held it up over my head just high enough in the middle of the opening to take a picture then put it up and got back to the business at hand. The perimeter held all night and throughout base camp as far as I could learn the next day.

The picture I took from this bunker I had not seen while I was looking through the slides that my wife's brother put on a CDROM and DVD. He had not included it, probably thinking it wasn't a good picture. Later I did find it but I almost didn't realize what I was looking at. It shows a line of muzzle flashes against a black background, from the perimeter, all the way across the middle of the picture with red tracers from the quad 50 machine guns going toward the perimeter from over the top of my bunker and the bunker to my left.

51
THE LAST PATROL

*"Though an army may encamp against me, my heart shall
not fear."*
—Psalms 27:3

I had been told that my orders to go home had come in
and I was due to leave for Cam Rhan on March 27, and fly
from there on March 28, 1968, to Fort Lewis, Wash. I was
due to go out on a patrol on March 7, which would be my
last patrol.

We left base camp the usual way, out the north road,
dropped off, radioed in, and headed east toward our first coordinate. We then headed south. TET was in full swing with
the base camp coming under attacks regularly. Our objective was to observe an enemy force, already determined to
be at least 3,000 strong, that had circled around east of the
base camp headed south and was expected to attack coming
up from the southeast. We were to continue south until we
reached an old banana plantation and wait there until an aerial observation could confirm the latest exact location of the
enemy.

They had earlier been reported as now moving in a northwest direction toward base camp but had stopped in a wood-
ed area. We waited for instructions because we sure didn't
need them to see us first. We were then given a coordinate to
move to that took us in a southeast direction and were told
to wait there. We were then less than 1,000 yards from the
wood line we were supposed to watch but felt we didn't have

a good view of enough of the area.

We realized that a slight rise we had passed about a 100 yards back gave us a better view. There was no movement to report so at dark we moved back to the rise we had passed and reported our move to base camp. They advised there would be an artillery barrage on the wood line at 4 a.m. unless we or one of the other patrols reported movement before then. This was the only time, that I know of, that we operated within our artillery range while observing the enemy.

We knew there was at least one other patrol east of the enemy and another south. We were also told that flares would be fired by artillery and air dropped over the wood line just before the barrage started. We were then to immediately report the direction of any movement made before and or after the barrage started. Our first surprise came just minutes before the barrage was to start with a mortar attack by the enemy on the area we had left. What prompted the attack at that precise time is a mystery, but we were sure glad we had moved. Our second surprise came from the barrage on the enemy when several rounds fell short around us and also around the area we left. Before we could get this corrected, several more rounds hit in our area but fortunately no one was killed.

We stayed at our position until dawn since we had no movement in our direction from the wood line; the flares continued all the while. About dawn we were told to move out northwest toward our pick-up point. As we were leaving, heading northwest to our pick-up point, we walked up on what I thought was a 155 round that had hit the ground, furrowed a ways under ground, then came up above ground and stopped on the ground about 30 yards behind our position. We skirted it quickly as one of the guys wrapped some toilet paper around a stick and stuck it in the ground near by to mark it. We also called in its location. It needed to be exploded so it wouldn't wind up being an enemy mine somewhere.

One of my earlier patrols could have been my last. While diligently trying to perform my duty of looking out for spider holes, pulling up the rear of the patrol, I lost sight of the last one or two men in the patrol. Panic. My first thought was to catch up quickly, but as my brain was now racing I also realized this could get me shot by my own men. I also knew I could not voice my delima and reveal our position. Other things raced through my mind, base camp was many miles to my right (west), it would be almost impossible to get through the base camp perimeter without a radio, than some reasoning finally set in. They would not change their direction until we reached the next coordinates on the map, and then they would wait until I caught up. I decided to just move a little quicker, as quietly as possible. Just as I was about to let my mind go racing off again, I caught sight of one of the men. Needless to say I never mention what had happened to anyone and no one asked me where I'd been. Sometimes, no matter what happens, how focused, cautious, alert, or whatever, you just know someone else is looking out for you.

3 t-Tango

52
STEAM BATH, SHOWER, AND MASSAGE

"My God will meet all your needs according to His glorious riches in Christ Jesus."
—Phil. 4:19

The best place to get really clean and relax was the steam bath, shower, and massage, managed and run by locals, located in the middle of 4th Division base camp. This may sound a little risqué but it was supervised by 4th Division personnel.

The way it was run reminded me of the YMCA. When you checked in you received a towel, a numbered card, and a numbered basket. However, when you left the shower or steam bath area you had to have your shorts on and your towel wrapped around you.

This place was best when I was covered with dust or dirt after riding in a convoy or out with S-5, also great after a patrol – fleas don't like steam baths – but good anytime you could find time and get in. It was always busy.

The first thing I'd do was take a shower then go sit in the steam room. After sitting in the steam for a while I'd take my plastic card, about 3 by 5 inches, and scrape it across my face and arms to see how much mud rolled up on the edge. It usually took at least three trips of shower then steam bath to get a fairly clean reading on the card.

Then I'd head for the massage room. It was a square room inside the main building with interior walls that did not go all the way up to the ceiling. There were small massage rooms all around the outside walls with a doorway in the inside wall opening into a hall, and more small rooms in the middle of the room opening out into the same hall. The hall was shaped like a U, with six rooms on the inside of the hall and about twelve on the outside. The office set in the opening of the U with the entrance on one side of the office and the exit on the other side. Each room had two massage tables, about waist high, except the office which had one, used when really busy, which was about all the time. Part of the massage was the girls walking around on your back – none of them looked like they weighed more than 80 pounds.

Since the walls didn't go to the ceiling, about four feet short, the girls talked to each other over the wall while they walked around on your back. The place sounded like a hen house because you couldn't understand any of what was said. The manager's name was Lein Lieb, she always checked everyone in. I usually got there late in the day when the place was full so sometimes she gave me a massage on the office massage table. The nine months I had been going there she always spoke and remembered my name. Her husband was an ARVN officer and she had a sister who also worked there.

The day after my last patrol I went there to get cleaned up, probably for the last time.

When I went in I realized the manager wasn't there and a GI officer was running the office. There weren't many people there, either. Lein's sister came up to me crying and said "My sister she dead, my sister she dead," and then ran back to where the other girls were standing. I asked one of the GIs standing at the door what happened. He said the manager and some other locals had been killed in their homes during a VC attack on March 8. I felt like I had lost a friend. A day or two later, Chuck and I took a jeep out to look at that area.

53
CAM RHAN TO HOME
March 28, 1968

I had less than three weeks to go at 1/22nd when I came off my last patrol. What I did those last three weeks I haven't a clue now. Did I check my DROS date on the mess hall wall? I'm sure I did. Did I send any more letters or audio cassettes home? I don't remember.

I remember running into Landis and meeting Bob Warden, a friend of Landis from 1/8th, in base camp when we were getting ready to leave for Cam Ranh. But I don't remember getting to Cam Ranh. I remember once we got there, there were five other guys in Cam Ranh, from Tiger-land, and one of them had a burned hand from some detail. We did get together and talk. One of the subjects was who had you seen

and what did you know about anybody from AIT. I had only seen Landis and Jimmy each once.

Landis told me when I saw him at the hospital that he knew of one of the guys who got killed during his first week in VN. Landis said he thought Jimmy was still alive but he wasn't on our flight home. I listened to the guys talking about some of the others who were from Tiger-land; they seemed to have been around some of the others in the field. The best I could gather was they knew of eight more who had made it, that made 14, and knew of 26 who didn't make it. That left 52 we didn't know anything about. Landis and I flew back on the same plane and vowed to keep in touch. That's all I remember about that flight.

54
INVISIBLE WOUNDS

When leaving Vietnam, my thoughts were of getting home and back to life as I remembered. However, we were told that not everyone had the same views as we did, so we knew things would be different. We were told to expect to be exposed to unfavorable remarks and news broadcasts about us and Vietnam. Now we were going to learn how things had changed back home.

But life had not stopped for us when we got off the plane in Vietnam to start up again when we got home. We knew that life in VN would be mentally and physically more intense than life had been at home and would require constant awareness of our environment and circumstances. We did not realize that we were never going to be the same again.

After returning home, we adjusted some to the new environment but it did not take much, like a news report, to take us back to that other world. Like a lot of soldiers, I didn't talk about my experiences, especially combat, except on some rare occasions with someone else who had been there, and on rarer occasions with a family member or very close friend. Some guys never talked about it at all. It was personal, private, and sometimes almost sacred to some.

It wasn't the physical experiences alone, you could express that, it was what you also experienced mentally. The emotional and psychological effect of combat experience cannot be adequately described in the written word. You had to be there and be part of it and feel it, you cannot feel it again nor convey that mental experience. The anxiety that can build from living day to day in a combat potential environment can only be understood by someone who has been there.

The "anxiety" increases as situations progress only to take second place in the heat of combat and then return after you have had time to assess the results and gain knowledge of your new circumstances. All involved can give a general description of what happened but each one has had a different mental experience.

Continual exposure to this kind of stress, especially when lives are lost, can have long-lasting effects (it can be seen in the eyes, at times for a while, by some, who know where it comes from), the "invisible wounds."

Tiger-land in 1967:
"If we could get you back in one year the person on each side of you would be missing."

"Only two people have ever offered to die for you: Jesus who died to provide salvation for your soul and the U.S. service people who died for your freedom."
—Author unknown

"The measure of love is what one is willing to give up for another."

P.S.: Landis and I are still "brothers"; we used to get together at least twice a year when he and his wife Elaine lived in Nashville and we lived in Hickory, N.C. We moved to the South Carolina coast in 1985 and they moved to the St. Louis area a few years before that. Now we call each other on birthdays and Christmas and whenever the mood strikes.

On one of my trips to Nashville, Landis and I drove down to Loretta, Tenn., to see Jimmy but after that it was just phone calls to him because we think it upset his wife for us to be there. He passed away several years ago. Landis often goes to the 4th Division reunions. I'm going to try to meet him there for the next one. Hope to see some of you there.

ALL GAVE SOME,
SOME GAVE ALL

GRAVES, GEORGE CALVIN IV

ARMY AUS Armor SGT(T)(See 30) E-5 26 Feb 68

Charlotte, North Carolina 9 Feb 42

31 18 42 55 LB #18 Newton, North Carolina 28659 10 Oct 66

Transferred to USAR (See 16) Fort Hood, Texas

Sec VI Ch 2 AR 635-200 SPN 201 Expiration of Term of Service 9 Oct 68
Trp F 3rd Sqdn 1st Cav 1st Armd Div HONORABLE None
Fort Hood Comd of Corps US Army Reserve (transferred)

Transferred to USAR Control Group (AnnIng) USAAC St Louis MO 63132 NE-1

9 Oct 72 NA NA NA NA

None E-1 Charlotte, North Carolina

1109 16th Ave., N.W. 2 0 0
Hickory (Catawba) North Carolina 28601 2 0 0
2 0 0
11840 Lt Inf 2 0 0
Infantryman NA USARPAC 0 11 26

National Defense Service Medal Combat Infantryman Badge Sharpshooter (Rifle)
Vietnam Service Medal w/3 Bronze Service Stars Expert (M-60 MG)
Republic of Vietnam Campaign Medal Marksman (Rifle M-16)

None

None NA NA

1 Year College Blood Group: O

Item 5a: PFC (T) E-3 Apld 21 Apr 67
Item 26b: Excess leave of 26 days from.

1109 16th Avenue N.W.
Hickory (Catawba) North Carolina 28601
THOMAS E. DUNLAP, 1LT, USA, Asst AG

DD Form 214 ARMED FORCES OF THE UNITED STATES
REPORT OF TRANSFER OR DISCHARGE 1

WHAT OTHERS ARE SAYING

"This story about your journey in Vietnam is very interesting. It keeps one's attention and is sincere and honest. I compliment you for taking the initiative to write it because it is from your heart. I know and understand how difficult it has been for you at times. It is well organized and the details are great, especially the ones when you were on patrols. The readers should get a good picture of you and Vietnam and they should understand you and what you are saying. I appreciate the loyalty and sincere interest you have shown me and I know our brother, Jim Pruitt, is smiling down on us for remembering him, too. Your follow-up on our AIT buddies in Tigerland is a touch of class.

Your story is something that needed to be done. It should finally help you with closure, rid you of the demons, and lift the burden you have carried for all of these years."

-- Landis Bargatze

A MESSAGE FROM THE AUTHOR

If you were there and were part of these events and have anything to add or change, or have an event of your own to relate, let me hear from you.

Relate who was involved, including names and units, etc., what, where, when, and why (or how) it happened. Include your name and address, phone number, rank, when you were in Vietnam, and your unit if not included in the event. Please also include a statement releasing material for my use.

Mail all of the above to me at P.O. Box 1333, Little River, South Carolina 29566

'......no man knows when his hour will come'.
Ecc. 9:12

Chopper pad

Base camp

View from my bunker/use stakes to point out movement

3 Tango

3 Tango

Recon

Tea Plantation

Pleiku Exp

Tea Plantation

Pleiku Exp

Flying high
and low

Pleiku area damage Mar. 8-68

Pleiku area damage Mar. 8-68

Base Camp damage Mar.8-68

Thanks

CPSIA information can be obtained
at www.ICGtesting.com
Printed in the USA
JSHW061910190622
27227JS00003B/87